How To Learn Mixed Martial Arts

Your Step By Step Guide To Learning Mixed Martial Arts

HowExpert with Nathan DeMetz

Copyright HowExpert™
www.HowExpert.com

For more tips related to this topic, visit HowExpert.com/mma.

Recommended Resources

- HowExpert.com – Quick 'How To' Guides on All Topics from A to Z by Everyday Experts.
- HowExpert.com/free – Free HowExpert Email Newsletter.
- HowExpert.com/books – HowExpert Books
- HowExpert.com/courses – HowExpert Courses
- HowExpert.com/clothing – HowExpert Clothing
- HowExpert.com/membership – HowExpert Membership Site
- HowExpert.com/affiliates – HowExpert Affiliate Program
- HowExpert.com/writers – Write About Your #1 Passion/Knowledge/Expertise & Become a HowExpert Author.
- HowExpert.com/resources – Additional HowExpert Recommended Resources
- YouTube.com/HowExpert – Subscribe to HowExpert YouTube.
- Instagram.com/HowExpert – Follow HowExpert on Instagram.
- Facebook.com/HowExpert – Follow HowExpert on Facebook.

COPYRIGHT, LEGAL NOTICE AND DISCLAIMER:

COPYRIGHT © BY HOWEXPERT™ (OWNED BY HOT METHODS). ALL RIGHTS RESERVED WORLDWIDE. NO PART OF THIS PUBLICATION MAY BE REPRODUCED IN ANY FORM OR BY ANY MEANS, INCLUDING SCANNING, PHOTOCOPYING, OR OTHERWISE WITHOUT PRIOR WRITTEN PERMISSION OF THE COPYRIGHT HOLDER.

DISCLAIMER AND TERMS OF USE: PLEASE NOTE THAT MUCH OF THIS PUBLICATION IS BASED ON PERSONAL EXPERIENCE AND ANECDOTAL EVIDENCE. ALTHOUGH THE AUTHOR AND PUBLISHER HAVE MADE EVERY REASONABLE ATTEMPT TO ACHIEVE COMPLETE ACCURACY OF THE CONTENT IN THIS GUIDE, THEY ASSUME NO RESPONSIBILITY FOR ERRORS OR OMISSIONS. ALSO, YOU SHOULD USE THIS INFORMATION AS YOU SEE FIT, AND AT YOUR OWN RISK. YOUR PARTICULAR SITUATION MAY NOT BE EXACTLY SUITED TO THE EXAMPLES ILLUSTRATED HERE; IN FACT, IT'S LIKELY THAT THEY WON'T BE THE SAME, AND YOU SHOULD ADJUST YOUR USE OF THE INFORMATION AND RECOMMENDATIONS ACCORDINGLY.

THE AUTHOR AND PUBLISHER DO NOT WARRANT THE PERFORMANCE, EFFECTIVENESS OR APPLICABILITY OF ANY SITES LISTED OR LINKED TO IN THIS BOOK. ALL LINKS ARE FOR INFORMATION PURPOSES ONLY AND ARE NOT WARRANTED FOR CONTENT, ACCURACY OR ANY OTHER IMPLIED OR EXPLICIT PURPOSE.

ANY TRADEMARKS, SERVICE MARKS, PRODUCT NAMES OR NAMED FEATURES ARE ASSUMED TO BE THE PROPERTY OF THEIR RESPECTIVE OWNERS, AND ARE USED ONLY FOR REFERENCE. THERE IS NO IMPLIED ENDORSEMENT IF WE USE ONE OF THESE TERMS.

NO PART OF THIS BOOK MAY BE REPRODUCED, STORED IN A RETRIEVAL SYSTEM, OR TRANSMITTED BY ANY OTHER MEANS: ELECTRONIC, MECHANICAL, PHOTOCOPYING, RECORDING, OR OTHERWISE, WITHOUT THE PRIOR WRITTEN PERMISSION OF THE AUTHOR.

ANY VIOLATION BY STEALING THIS BOOK OR DOWNLOADING OR SHARING IT ILLEGALLY WILL BE PROSECUTED BY LAWYERS TO THE FULLEST EXTENT. THIS PUBLICATION IS PROTECTED UNDER THE US COPYRIGHT ACT OF 1976 AND ALL OTHER APPLICABLE INTERNATIONAL, FEDERAL, STATE AND LOCAL LAWS AND ALL RIGHTS ARE RESERVED, INCLUDING RESALE RIGHTS: YOU ARE NOT ALLOWED TO GIVE OR SELL THIS GUIDE TO ANYONE ELSE.

THIS PUBLICATION IS DESIGNED TO PROVIDE ACCURATE AND AUTHORITATIVE INFORMATION WITH REGARD TO THE SUBJECT MATTER COVERED. IT IS SOLD WITH THE UNDERSTANDING THAT THE AUTHORS AND PUBLISHERS ARE NOT ENGAGED IN RENDERING LEGAL, FINANCIAL, OR OTHER PROFESSIONAL ADVICE. LAWS AND PRACTICES OFTEN VARY FROM STATE TO STATE AND IF LEGAL OR OTHER EXPERT ASSISTANCE IS REQUIRED, THE SERVICES OF A PROFESSIONAL SHOULD BE SOUGHT. THE AUTHORS AND PUBLISHER SPECIFICALLY DISCLAIM ANY LIABILITY THAT IS INCURRED FROM THE USE OR APPLICATION OF THE CONTENTS OF THIS BOOK.

COPYRIGHT BY HOWEXPERT™ (OWNED BY HOT METHODS)
ALL RIGHTS RESERVED WORLDWIDE.

Table of Contents

Recommended Resources 2
Introduction: What is MMA? 7
    Before We Begin 7
    What is MMA? 8
    The History of MMA 8
    What Are You Going To Learn? 9
Section 1: Stand-up Striking 11
    The Basic Staggered Stance for Striking 12
    The Basic Staggered Stance for Movement 15
    Striking with Punches 17
    A Quick Word about Defense 27
    Simple Punch Combos for MMA 28
    1-2-3-4 (jab-cross-front hook-rear hook) combo (not pictured) 28
    Jab Combos: 1-1 (jab-jab) and the 1-1-2 (jab-jab-cross) plus variations (not pictured) 28
    Upper-Lower Combos 29
    Head hook, body hook 30
    Basic Kicks for MMA 34
    Front Round-Kick 40
    Simple Kick Combos MMA 44
    Teep to Rear Round-kick 44
    Front Round-Kick to Rear Round-Kick 47
    1-2 to Round-Kick 50
    Other Kicks 52
    Knee Strikes for MMA 52
    Uses for Knees in MMA 56
    A Quick Reminder about Safety 56
    Elbows 56
    Round Elbow 57
    The Downward Elbow 59
    Knee and Elbow Combos 63
    1-2 (Jab-Cross) to Front Elbow 64
    Other Knees and Elbows 66

Section Review 67
Section 2: The Clinch 68
  Establishing the Head-Clinch 68
  Establishing the Body-Clinch 73
  Punches and Elbows from the Head-Clinch 76
  Elbow from the Head-Clinch 77
  Uppercut to Head from Head-Clinch 79
  Uppercut to the Body from Head-Clinch 81
  Hook to Body from Head-Clinch 83
  Knees from the Head-Clinch 84
  Straight Knees to the Gut from Head-Clinch (not pictured) 85
  Straight Knees to the Head from Clinch (Not Pictured) 85
  The Thai Snake 86
  The Push-Off From the Head-Clinch 89
  Other Techniques from the Head-Clinch 92
  Strikes from the Body-Clinch 92
  Takedowns from the Body-Clinch 93
  Body-Clinch to Double-Leg 94
  Body-Clinch to Single-Leg 98
  Body-Clinch to Back Control to Takedown 101
  Simple Clinch Combos for MMA 104
  1-2, Head-Clinch to Straight Knees to Double-Leg (Not Pictured) 104
  Jab to Body-Clinch to Back Control to Rear-Takedown to Rear Naked Choke (Not Pictured) .. 105
  Other Combos 105
  Section Review 106
Section 3: Takedowns 107
  Double-Leg Rakedown 107
  Single-Leg 111
  Trips, Throws, and Other Takedowns 115
  Takedown Defense 115
  Palm-Stop and Forearm-Stop 116
  The Knee to the Face (Not Pictured) 120

- Guillotine Counter (Not Pictured) 120
- Go Heavy 120
- Other Takedown Defense 121
- Section 4: Grappling 122
  - Controlling the Opponent 122
  - Wrist Control 123
  - Head and Arm Control 128
  - Passing the Guard 131
  - Submissions and Ground-and-Pound 132
  - The Lead In 133
  - Elbows From Mount-Top 138
  - Americana from Mount 140
  - Mounted Crucifix to Punches and Elbows 144
  - Other Submissions from Side-Control and Top-Mount 148
  - Arm Bar from Guard 149
  - Grappling Combos 161
- The End 163
  - Just the Beginning 164
- Recommended Resources 167

Introduction: What is MMA?

Before We Begin

Hi. Since you are reading this book, you clearly have an interest in learning more about MMA. As a personal trainer and a person who loves/practices martial arts, I want to help you learn. It is always nice to give something back.

Before we start, I want to note a few things: I have several other books out, all created on behalf of the publisher and distributed by them. Some of them have drawn criticism. I want to address that. I do not claim to be the best instructor nor do I think I am.

Are there better teachers who have been doing this longer? Yes there are. I do not expect to make an MMA master out of you through text and pictures. My goal is to inform you on how to do some basic techniques and show you how to put them together for MMA.

My name is not Greg Jackson, Rener Gracie, or Jon Jones. I am simply a man who enjoys what he does and is trying to share it with you. If you want to learn some basics of MMA, read on. If you expect perfection or expect this text to mirror every other trainer's style and delivery, then you will be disappointed. I do not think I am perfect. We are all different in our styles of teaching. I respect that other practitioners differ in their views and I accept their input to grow better. Can you say the same? If you can enter with an open an unbiased mind, please read on. If not, then this text may not be the best for you and I wish you the best in your teachings elsewhere. Let us begin then, shall we?

What is MMA?

MMA is an acronym for mixed martial arts. It references a stylized type of training and method of fighting. It is by default a combination of methods, including stand-up striking, clinch work, and grappling, among other aspects. As time goes on, the shift from traditional single art forms to mixed martial arts is occurring. In this manner, MMA is becoming less of a combination of other arts and more an art unto itself. The fighters seen in MMA rings are increasingly people who trained mixed martial arts their entire career/life instead of learning one traditional art, then another, and so on.

The History of MMA

This history of mixed martial arts goes back further than anyone can remember. The reason for this is that any time a person learns two martial arts and combines them into one skill base; this person has effectively become a mixed marital artist.

Now, many people see the beginnings of mixed martial arts as occurring in response to the Ultimate Fighting Championships (UFC). This is simply not true. Martial artists such as Bruce Lee and others practiced multiple forms of martial arts and combined them into one skill base, long before the concept of the UFC came to be. This makes them mixed martial artists.

However, it is true that mixed martial arts grew in popularity as the UFC grew. Today, it is the flagship for the mixed martial arts community. Virtually every competitive mixed martial artist seeks to be a part of the UFC. Just remember that MMA goes back further than the UFC.

What Are You Going To Learn?

Well, I am not going to bore with an endless history lesson. That is for sure. I am excited to share with you the process for combining styles into a mixed martial arts base. True to MMA, I will combine all aspects of fighting, albeit in limited detail due to the textual constraints of this manual.

This manual does not teach you each of the different arts in extreme detail. Instead, I am assuming that you have a working knowledge, even if it is a limited one, of the martial arts reviewed and combined here. To teach you each of the martial arts is beyond the scope of this text. This text will instead begin teaching you how to combine them in an effective manner. This can be for the purpose of fun, fitness, ring fighting, or self-defense. If you need more information on the kickboxing and jiu-jitsu techniques performed in this manual, How To Expert published two other manuals from me that cover these techniques in detail: "How to Jiu-jitsu for beginners" and "How to Kickbox for beginners".

Now I do not condone fighting outside of the ring. While I have no problem with two people 'getting down', then shaking hands and walking way, that is just *not* the way things happen most of the time. No longer, can two men or two women engage in a simple fight and that be the end of it. Nowadays, people go to jail or someone comes back with a gun. For this reason, I do not condone fighting in the streets and instead suggest resolving problems in a non-violent way.

Regardless, with enough practice, the techniques you learn here will allow you to effectively stand-up strike with an opponent, take them to the ground, defend from both positions, and submit a person or perform ground-and-pound. This manual will be broken down as follows:

Section 1 - Stand-up striking: This section will review kicks, punches, knees, and elbows used as attacks from a standing position and illustrate how to combine these strikes.

Section 2 – Clinch: This section will offer an introduction to the clinch. Covered are both the head-clinch and the body-clinch/underhooks. Included are strikes and defensive work from these positions as well as takedowns.

Section 3 – Takedowns: This will cover takedowns.

Section 4 – Grappling: This section offers users ideas for what to do in various positions on the ground. Covered are top and bottom positions focusing on striking, defense and submissions.

Section 1: Stand-up Striking

Stand-up striking refers to the art of striking and defending against strikes from a standing position. Each striking art has a set stance or series of stances, as well as a specific style of movement that is used. My background is in boxing and Muay Thai, although there are techniques from Taekwondo and other arts included in my skill set.

The first thing that a person learns in stand-up striking is stance. Stance includes foot placement, knee bend, hand positioning, and head positioning. Each stand-up art has a different type of stance or multiple stances. I use a basic staggered stance that is applicable for MMA and striking. There are two variations: the striking stance and the movement stance. I also commonly use the side stance. There are other stances incorporated from time to time, but these are the basic stances that I use. For this manual, I will use an orthodox, or right-handed, stance. The techniques apply to a southpaw, or a left-handed stance, as well, simply in reverse positioning.

The Basic Staggered Stance for Striking

Figure 1: This is the basic staggered stance that I use when striking. The hand position is high to the face for protection. I am looking forward at my opponent. My hips point at an angle, as does my rear foot. My front foot is forward, although a slight angle is okay. From here, I can roll my punches and deliver power. This stance allows for solid kicking with the rear leg and allows for kick checking (blocking) with the front leg.

Figure 2: This is the side shot of that same position.

Figure 3: Opposite side shot of the basic staggered stance used for striking.

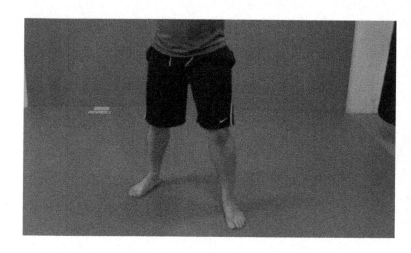

Figure 4: A close-up shot of the foot positioning.

The Basic Staggered Stance for Movement

Figure 5: The basic staggered stance for movement is a position in which a person is on the balls of their feet and light on their feet. This allows quick movement and facilitates evasion and stick-and-move type tactics. The stance is narrower than the basic staggered stance for striking. The reason for this is that it allows ease of movement. A person can move with the striking stance; but this person uses a type of plodding that does not facilitate quickness or ease of movement. While I do use plodding at some points, when it is time to move quickly and efficiently I am light on my feet.

Figure 6: Side shot of the basic staggered stance for movement.

Figure 7: Other side shot for the basic staggered stance for movement.

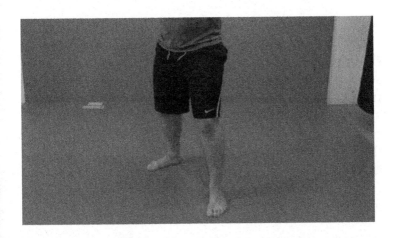

Figure 8: Close-up shot of foot position. Note the difference from this stance and the more squared striking stance.

To learn more about stance, you can watch the video appropriately titled "Basic Stance" and for more about movement you can watch this video. YouTube hosts the videos but they are also available on my website, nathandemetz.com.

Striking with Punches

A punch is the most basic strike there is. In most stand-up striking arts, some form of the punch is the first strike that a person will learn. Variations abound and, for the purpose of this manual, I will be using a boxing method of punching stylized for MMA and kickboxing. The primary focus for punching is the six basic punches: jab, cross, front hook, rear hook, front uppercut, and rear uppercut.

Notice that I do not denote punches as left and right, but rather front and rear. The reason for this is that the punches change based on orthodox or southpaw stance. For example, the left straight punch from the orthodox stance is the jab, while the left straight punch from southpaw is the cross. Front and rear are universal terms. If I say rear, you know to throw with your rear hand; if I say front you know to throw with your front hand. For ease of learning, regardless of stance, I prefer these terms when I train folks.

The Straight Punches: Jab and the Cross

Figure 9: The jab starts from our basic staggered stance for striking. Notice my hands held high, my gaze forward, and my chin tucked.

Figure 10: The jab comes straight out from the body. Notice that the back of my hand faces upwards, my gaze is forward, my chin is tucked, and my shoulder turned over to facilitate the full range of the punch.

Figure 11: Return to start position. Remember that the hand should not stay extended for long. As quickly as the punch goes out is as quick as it should return to the start position.

Figure 12: The cross comes from the basic staggered stance for striking, same as the jab.

Figure 13: The cross comes straight out from the body. Notice that the back of my hand is rotated upwards, my gaze is forward, my chin is tucked, and my shoulder turned over to facilitate the full range of the punch.

Figure 14: Return to the start position.

The Hooks: Front and Rear

Figure 15: The hooks comes from the basic staggered stance for striking, same as the straight punches.

Figure 16: The hook travels slightly upward and across, in the process of aiming for an opponent's cheek. To begin the front hook, there will be a rear rotation of the body and a slight dip of the shoulder/arm - pictured here.

Figure 17: The top position of the arm should be near parallel or parallel to the ground. In this image, I am near parallel. This is the front hook, since I am in an orthodox stance.

Figure 18: The rear hook starts from the same position as the front hook and rotates in much the same way. You will have a greater path to travel, since it starts further back.

Figure 19: In this image, I have thrown the rear hook. It is in the top position and parallel to the ground.

Figure 20: I return to the start position.

Uppercuts: Front and Rear

Figure 21: This is the starting position for the uppercut. It is the same as the starting position for all the other punches.

Figure 22: The uppercut travels upward and in, as you aim for the opponent's chin. To begin the front uppercut, there will be a rear rotation of the body and a slight dip of the shoulder/arm - pictured here

Figure 23: As my body rotates forward, my front hand moves slightly out from my body and arcs in an angle toward the face. It does not come right up the middle, but rather

travels at an angle, with my target the chin of my opponent.

Figure 24: The rear shot moves in the same way. The rear uppercut starts from the same position as the front hook and rotates in much the same way. You will have a greater path to travel since it starts from further back.

Figure 25: Return to the start position.

Any of these punches can attack an opponent's face or body. I am not illustrating the body punches here, since, as I mentioned in the beginning, I am assuming you have a previous base in striking. This is simply a quick review, so that you know the moves that will be included when we get to the meat of the manual.

A Quick Word about Defense

You will notice that a section on defense is missing from here. This is due to two reasons: 1) textual limitations by the publisher and 2) the assumption that you already have a basic knowledge of boxing and defensive maneuvers. If you do not, then I suggest you look over How to Kickbox for Beginners or another book or series of videos that review: how to Pillar, Bob-and-weave, Rock-back, Hook-block, and other defensive maneuvers such as evasion.

The point of this text is not to give you an in-depth view of all the various martial arts moves included here, but rather to give you an idea of how to combine them into one cohesive art known as mixed martial arts. The reviews I offered above specifically relate to combinations and techniques used further on in the manual.

Simple Punch Combos for MMA

All right, here we are. Now that we have done a quick review of the basic punches for boxing and kickboxing, we can get into some moderate combos for MMA. Since I am assuming you know basic combos such as the 1-2 combo and double hooks, I will pass those over. Let us start with the 1-2-3-4 or the jab-cross-front hook-rear hook.

1-2-3-4 (jab-cross-front hook-rear hook) combo (not pictured)

This is a basic combo. You should have learned it early on in boxing and possibly kickboxing, depending on the focus of the teacher. Regardless, you can get a feel for it here. Start in stance, a little more squared up for striking. Throw the jab. As the jab comes back to start, throw the cross. As the cross comes back to start, throw the front hook and follow with the rear hook. It is that simple in thought, though this combo can take some to perfect.

Jab Combos: 1-1 (jab-jab) and the 1-1-2 (jab-jab-cross) plus variations (not pictured)

The jab has to be the best set up punch, if not the best set up strike. Properly used it can get an opponent off-balance and make an opening for something bigger. It can also inflict a lot of damage when paired with enough force and accuracy. Start in stance a little less square. Throw the jab out and then pull the jab back, but stop short of returning to start position, before throwing out the jab again. This combo can be used to push forward, to close distance for another strike or takedown/clinch. This is ideal, if you prefer dirty boxing or takedowns and submissions.

You can incorporate many variations with the double jab. A hook, uppercut, or even a kick can follow the jab-jab. You can follow it up with multiple techniques, such as the cross then the front hook. You can use this technique to apply pressure, or even defensively to move out of a corner or side step. Be creative.

Upper-Lower Combos

One of the best approaches to keeping an opponent off-balance is to mix up striking. A common way to do this is to use upper-lower combos. Upper-lower combos can be head, then body shots or punches, then kicks/knees.

Head hook, body hook

Figure 26: Start in stance.

Figure 27: Throw the front hook to the head...

Figure 28: Then the rear hook to the body.

Front hook to body, front hook to head

Figure 29: Start in stance...

Figure 30: Throw the hook to the body...

Figure 31: then instead of returning completely to start, torque the body again...

Figure 32: and quickly throw the hook to the head. When done right, this catches the opponent off guard, leaving them open for the knockout. While all combos require speed and technique, this one truly does. To catch the opponent off guard, this has to done quick and tight.

Now these are a couple of simple examples and are far from all combo types. One of my personal favorites to throw is upper-lower-lower-upper hooks, meaning front head hook, followed by rear body hook, followed by front body hook, followed by rear head hook. I could go one with others, but the point is that variety is key. Practice throwing different combos together. You can do this with straight shots, such as the jab to head followed by the cross to the body or mix straight punches with hooks, such as the jab to the head then the hook to the body.

Basic Kicks for MMA

Let us change focus from punches to kicks. Many different kicks find use in MMA. I am going to keep things simple and focus on just three kicks. Each is relatively easy to learn and can be incorporated into combos. What follows next is a quick review of a kickboxing style: rear round-kick, teep, and front round-kick.

The Round-kick or Roundhouse Kick

Figure 33: The kick begins in the basic striking stance.

Figure 34: The body rotates toward the target as the kicking side arm comes down as a counter-balance.

Figure 35: The body is in mid-kick in this image about to make contact with the target.

Figure 36: The kick has connected with the target. Notice that my shin is connecting with the bag, not my foot or ankle. This is ideal.

Figure 37: Return to start position.

Figure 38: The round-kick was delivered to thigh level, in the last image. This kick can be thrown to the body and to the head as well.

Figure 39: In this image, the kick connects at head level. Notice that due to the extension of my leg to achieve height, I am kicking with my instep, which is the area where my ankle and foot meet. When kicking at the end of your leg striking range, this will be ideal, as it will be

impossible to make contact with your shin to the opponent's head.

Figure 40: Return to start position.

The Teep (Push-kick)

Figure 41: The kick begins in the basic striking stance. In this series of photos, I am going to target the BOB practice dummy.

Figure 42: I am kicking with the rear leg, so I must bring that leg forward. As the leg comes forward, the knee raises in an upward direction while I begin to lean back.

Figure 43: I then push straight out, using my leg muscles, specifically the quadriceps, as well as the forward motion of my hips to drive the ball of my foot into the target. Although

generally used as a defensive maneuver, this kick can inflict damage as well. Generally, the kick ends with a step through, where you will find your kicking leg is now your font leg.

However, when practicing against a target such as BOB or a bag on the wall, as pictured in the back, you will need to draw your front foot back to the start position.

Front Round-Kick

The front round-kick can be performed in a number of ways. One common example is the snap round-kick seen in arts such as karate or taekwondo. It relies on the snap of the knee for its power and therefore lacks in power. The switch round-kick is common in Muay Thai and similar arts. A quick change of stance in which you pop your front leg back facilitates your movement. Off the switch, you then perform the round-kick in the opposite stance. This creates greater power in the kick, but is an obvious maneuver, which is easier for opponents to block. Instead of those kicks, we will focus on performing the front round-kick from your normal stance and over-torqueing the hips.

Figure 44: The kick starts from your normal stance. Like the rear round-kick, you will use the rotation of your hips to drive the kick to the target.

Figure 45: In this image, you see that I have started to lean to my right and am beginning to draw the leg up. There is no switch, although my rear foot does slide up.

Figure 46: This image shows me further along in the process. My non-kicking foot and ankle have rotated my body to facilitate the movement of the kick. My arm has fallen as a counter-balance and I am leaning back.

Figure 47: The kick hits its target, which is in this case the ribs.

Figure 48: Return to the start position.

Simple Kick Combos MMA

All right, here we are again. Now that we have done a quick review of the basic kicks for kickboxing, we can get into some simple kick combos for MMA. These are combos that I personally find effective and, that should be relatively easy to master, with appropriate practice. This is of course assuming you already have some experience with the kicks.

Teep to Rear Round-kick

This combo pushes the opponent off-balance and then connects with the body, head, or leg to cause damage. The teep should hit the gut, while the round-kick may go to the thigh, ribs/gut, or to the head.

Figure 49: Start in your basic stance...

Figure 50: Lift the front knee...

Figure 51: Push the front foot straight out into the opponents gut...

Figure 52: Let the front foot come straight down in front of you, then immediately rotate your hips to begin the round-kick.

Figure 53: Follow through with the round-kick, shown at about rib/gut level in this image. If you connect, draw your leg back to start position. If you miss, follow through and step/spin out from the kick, landing with your guard up, in case the opponent looks to counter.

Front Round-Kick to Rear Round-Kick

This combo is great for causing damage to the body, head or legs. For example, the first kick may target the inside of the front leg, while the second targets the outside. Running with that example, imagine the heavy bag in the images below is the front leg of an opponent.

Figure 54: Start in the basic stance.

Figure 55: Throw the front kick to the inside of the leg. This can cause immediate pain and slow down an opponent's movement.

Figure 56: Draw the front kick back and immediately follow with the rear.

Figure 57: Allow the rear to hit the outside of the leg. This can cause immediate damage and slow the opponent's movement. The front and back round-kicks together can cause severe damage quickly, when delivered with enough accuracy and power.

Vary this combo by changing the targets. For example, deliver both kicks to the rib/gut area. You can deliver front round-kick to the inside of the thigh, and then back round-kick to the ribs. You could deliver the front round-kick to the inside of the thigh, and then aim for the head with the back round-kick. Be creative and find combos that work for you.

1-2 to Round-Kick

Figure 58: Start in the basic stance...

Figure 59: Throw the jab...

Figure 60: Followed by the cross…

Figure 61: The cross returns to start position. A brief pause occurs, and then you rotate the hips to deliver the round-kick.

Other Kicks

As noted, I am not going to offer a complete tutorial on each aspect of MMA, but rather an overview of specific areas and ways to throw it all together. However, I will offer thoughts about other elements that can be included. Here are some thoughts on other kicks that may be useful for MMA:

Switch kick – This kick can be effective for MMA when timed properly. The striker does a quick switch-step, which makes the front leg the back leg. The kick comes off the new "back leg".

Sidekick – This kick can be thrown off the front or rear leg. The striker must throw the kick from the side stance. An illustration of this technique is available in "How to: Kickbox for Beginners".

Knee Strikes for MMA

A knee strike from a standing position works as both an attacking movement and a defensive maneuver.

Figure 62: This is starting position for the knee. I will begin with the rear leg. As you throw the knee, it travels upward at an angle away from your body.

Figure 63: This first knee attacks thigh level. The use of this knee is less common, but finds use to strike someone's thigh as they throw a punch and you Rock-back to avoid. It is also common from the clinch.

Figure 64: This second knee reaches about crotch level. Clearly, this may strike someone in the crotch, although not in a ring fight. Additionally it can be used to knee-strike the head of an opponenet who is attempting a double-leg takedown.

Figure 65: This final knee reaches about gut/diaphragm height of a person between 5'8 to 6'0.

Figure 66: After any of these knees, you can return to the start position by drawing your leg back. However, you can also drive forward and land with your attacking leg forward. This can set you up for other moves such as following the knee with elbows or punches.

Uses for Knees in MMA

Any of these knees may attack from the basic stance. Any time an opponent moves in, but is too close for a punch or kick, the knee may be used. If an opponent reaches for your head to establish the clinch, you can knee them. If an opponent shoots in for a double-leg takedown, you can knee them. At this point, I am not going to do a deep review of knees. I generally feel that there are better techniques in most situations that may call for a knee.

A Quick Reminder about Safety

Safety is essential. While throwing blows at full strength might seem like fun, they are not fun when you are on the receiving end. The knee to the face is especially dangerous as hard contact can result in a knockout, broken nose, black eye, broken jaw, shattered orbital socket, and... I think you get the point. Practice with safety in mind. Save the power for the ring or the street. With a blow like this, I recommend tippy-tapping unless working on a bag or pad.

Elbows

When striking with the elbow, the idea is to hit the target with the tip, or point, of the elbow. It can inflict the most damage and may result in a cut or knockout to the opponent. The following series of images offers a quick review of the round, downward, and upward elbows.

Round Elbow

Figure 67: The round elbow is the most basic of all elbows. It travels across the face parallel to the ground. The ideal target for this elbow is the jaw line or the cheekbone. The start position is the standard striking stance.

Figure 68: The elbow travels at an upward angle until it reaches the right height...

Figure 69: then travels across the target...

Figure 70: before returning to the start position.

The Downward Elbow

Figure 71: The start position for the downward elbow.

Figure 72: Although named the downward elbow, it must first travel to the proper height... similar ...

Figure 73: to that of the round elbow....

Figure 74: before striking downward at the opponent's face...

Figure 75: and returning to the start position. The exact target for this elbow may be the forehead, eye, or jaw. This elbow can be slightly more devastating than the round elbow due to the downward force of the body behind it.

Upward Elbow

Figure 76: The upward elbow starts in the same position as the round and the downward elbows.

Figure 77: The upward elbow simply travels at an upward angle...

Figure 78: To strike the opponent in the jaw. It is arguably the easiest elbow to throw since it does not need to reach height before striking. However, it does not have the same power as the round elbow or the downward elbow.

Knee and Elbow Combos

To be honest, you are probably not going to use knee combos often, except from the clinch. Even then, it will not be a common move unless you tend to work in the clinch on a regular basis. We will go over that in the clinch section, which is the next section. The same is true for elbows. Most times if you stay in that close to a person, it is advisable to clinch up or back out as they are going to be looking to strike you too. Combine that with the awkwardness some people feel when throwing elbows, let alone combining with them, and this lends more to the thought that combos with elbows, and knees for the matter, will be rare, or at least reserved for people who are highly skilled with them. Other people may disagree with me on this and that is fine. This is my personal opinion based on my own practice, teaching others, and watching/learning from others. For this reason, I will not include knee and elbow combos, per se. Instead, I will include a short combo that ends with an elbow off punches.

1-2 (Jab-Cross) to Front Elbow

Figure 79: This combo begins from the basic stance. Your hands are high protecting your face.

Figure 80: You begin with the jab...

Figure 81: follow with the cross, moving in as you do...

Figure 82: then end with the front elbow, before returning to stance. This combo is ideal for times when you have closed the distance with the 1-2. It will take some practice getting the movement/distance just right. Practice with a partner to get it right. Additionally, this combination leads into the head-clinch.

Other Knees and Elbows

Other knees and elbows that may include the flying knee, spinning back elbow, and rear elbows. Each has its merit. However, the flying knee takes skill to perfect and is normally a low-percentage move. The spinning round elbow is the same. The back elbows are only useful if someone has taken your back from a standing or ground position and you have space to use them.

Section Review

In this section, you have received a quick review about strikes. You have also been shown a few combos that are easy to learn and, with practice, easy to master. This is not, by any means, all-inclusive of the combinations or techniques available in stand-up striking. I encourage further learning, whether from the previously mentioned kickboxing manual or from another source. When practicing the above individual techniques and combos, think of ways to mix it up. Some of the combos that I most prefer today are ones I played with and found to be just right for me. Do not be afraid to be creative. However, if you find that combinations seem awkward or, I dare say, dangerous to perform and practice will not correct it, perhaps you should not perform it. Additionally you can review this [this video](#) for further help with technique on the jab, cross, and 1-2 combo and [this video](#) for a quick example of the round-kick.

Section 2: The Clinch

The clinch is an often-misunderstood position in many martial arts. One cannot ignore its importance to MMA. The clinch is a position in which you have locked your arms/hands around an opponent's head or body. The purpose of the clinch is to gain control of the opponent's body. In doing so, you can control where they move, stifle their attacks and, launch your own attacks.

For the clinch, I will offer more than just a review. The reason for this is that, depending on whom you trained under for kickboxing and jiu-jitsu, this area may have been skipped or taught in minimal detail. For MMA you will need at least a basic understanding of the clinch.

Establishing the Head-Clinch

The first area to cover is establishing the clinch. The head-clinch is common to stand-up arts such as Muay Thai or kickboxing, while the body-clinch is common to grappling arts such as judo or jiu-jitsu. Both have benefits applicable to MMA.

Figure 83: As noted, you can establish the clinch in two ways: by grabbing the head or the body. We will start with the head. Establishing the head-clinch in MMA is ideal, if you want to work dirty boxing, attempt a submission from the clinch, or to initiate a takedown from the clinch.

Figure 84: To this end a person begins in the striking position, as that is where all fights begin. From here, you can throw punches to

move in toward the opponent while they defend.

Figure 85: In this example, we will use the 1-2 combo. See her throwing the 1 ...

Figure 86: Now see her throwing the 2. You are throwing the 1-2 to get the opponent to

block. This is to prevent them from avoiding the head grab.

Figure 87: You immediately throw another 1, the jab...

Figure 88: then fake as if you are going to throw the 2, the cross. Instead, use your rear hand to reach outside of the opponents guard to establish the clinch. Inside is better, but outside can be easier to establish. It can be a strong position as well, especially if you have solid grip, arm, and back strength.

8Figure 89: In this image, my training partner has established the head-clinch.

Establishing the Body-Clinch

Generally, when I talk about the body-clinch I am referring to having your arms wrapped around the opponent in a bear hug kind of fashion. You can be high and in close with your arms under the armpits, or you can have arms wrapped around the waist, while your body is lower to the ground and your feet pushed further back. Conversely, you can have you arms anywhere between the two points.

Now what you see in MMA a lot are the underhooks. This is essentially the high body-clinch position with your arms up under the armpits, turned upwards, and the hands cupping the back/shoulders. I do not focus a lot on this position; nor have the people I learned from and trained with. The reason for this is that action from this position dictates that you change position. For example, if you are going to slam someone, you are not going to slam him or her with underhooks. Instead, you are going to get a firm grip around their body, pick them up, and slam them into the ground. This is not to say that I will not use the underhooks or over-under, but that they are not my go-to and the moves I example here rely on the other clinch techniques.

Figure 90: To establish the body-clinch, we begin in the same manner as we would for the head-clinch, from the striking position.

Figure 91: The goal here is a little different from that for the head-clinch. With the head-clinch, we needed a more intricate distraction to gain entry to the head. For the body-clinch, we simply need to get the hands of the opponent up in a defensive position. To do this throw the jab.

Figure 92: Once the opponent brings their hand to the head, shoot in for the body-clinch. While moving forward you change levels by dropping down, extending your arms as you move in.

Figure 93: Reach your arms around the opponent, as if you gave them a bear hug.

Figure 94: The handgrip you use to grasp the opponent can vary. You can use hand-on-wrist, palm-to-palm, and cup-grip (hand-over-hand).

Punches and Elbows from the Head-Clinch

From the head-clinch, it is possible to throw strikes to the head and body. You can use punches, elbows, and knees.

Elbow from the Head-Clinch

Figure 95: Start with the head-clinch established.

Figure 96: With the inside head-clinch you will pull back the arm with which you want to strike, while holding onto the head firmly with the opposite hand.

Figure 97: Drive the elbow toward the face of the opponent. You can target the forehead, eye, or jaw. As you drive the elbow forward, try to pull the head of the opponent toward you. This allows you to maintain control; helps prevent evasion by the opponent and, can create a stronger strike.

Ideally, you are going to stick with elbows from this position. However, if you want to throw a punch you need to understand how to. You are not going to draw back as you did with the elbow and try to throw a straight shot. Instead, you are going to use the uppercut to the jaw or the uppercut or hook to the body.

Uppercut to Head from Head-Clinch

Figure 98: This is the start position.

Figure 99: Let us start with the upper cut to the head. From the head-clinch, draw one hand free. Drop the arm and shoulder, being sure to keep a tight hold of the opponent with the other hand.

Figure 100: Drive the uppercut upward. It is a short shot. In idea, this is a simple technique.

However, like all moves, the technique can take time to learn effectively.

Uppercut to the Body from Head-Clinch

Figure 101: Next, we move into the uppercut to the body. It will travel essentially at the same angle as the standard uppercut to the body normally does.

Figure 102: Drop your hand down from the opponent's head and draw it back to your body.

Figure 103: Drive the punch forward and upward, aiming for the diaphragm or solar plexus. This target is ideal as it can knock the air from the opponent.

Hook to Body from Head-Clinch

Figure 104: Next, we move into the hook to the body. It will travel essentially at the same angle as the standard hook to the body normally does.

Figure 105: Drop one hand down from the opponent's head and draw it back to your body and slightly outward.

Figure 106: Drive the punch inward in an arching motion, as if you were throwing the traditional hook to the body. Aim for the ribs or liver, depending on which side of the body you are targeting.

Knees from the Head-Clinch

Knees from the head-clinch, in my opinion, take greater skill than the punches or elbows. Learning how to position yourself and balance while throwing knees can be difficult for some. At least, with the elbows and punches, your feet are still on the ground. However, knees from the clinch can be effective in MMA based fighting. There are a number of knees used, but I am going to keep it simple and focus on the straight knees from the clinch to body.

Straight Knees to the Gut from Head-Clinch (not pictured)

The straight knees to the gut are performed much in the same manner as rear knee to the thigh. You simply have to aim higher and change the body mechanics a bit. Start in the clinch with your hand positioning on the inside. Create space by taking a quick step back and then drive the rear knee in an upward and forward direction, while simultaneously pulling the opponent toward you, then return to the start position.

Straight Knees to the Head from Clinch (Not Pictured)

Now these may be the most fun knees to perform. There is something special about kneeing another person in the face. Trust me; it's no fun to be on the other end. These knees are especially dangerous, much in the way the knee to stop the double-leg is. Be careful and practice at a comfortable speed that allows proficient movement, but does not leave someone excessively open to catching a knee to the face.

Start with the inside head-clinch. Step your attacking leg back, as needed, to create space and then drive the knee upward and forward as you pull the person's face down toward your knee, before returning to start position. Conversely, you can pull the person's head to the side and drive your knee up at an angle.

The Thai Snake

The Thai Snake derives its name from the art of Muay Thai. You may or may not find a lot of use for it in the MMA game or street. However, I feel it is an important technique; one that I would not want to be without. Simply put, the Thai Snake is fighting for positional control. Whenever you have the head-clinch, the strongest position is the inside position. The Thai Snake helps you achieve it when the opponent has the inside clinch.

Figure 107: The Thai Snake starts from the head-clinch position. You will need a partner. Give your partner the inside clinch and establish the outside clinch yourself, as shown in the image.

Figure 108: From here, release one hand from the neck of your partner, bring your hand and arm to the inside of your partner's clinch...

Figure 109: then push your hand up to the side of their head and establish the inside clinch with that hand.

Figure 110: You now have the inside clinch with this hand. To establish the inside clinch with the other hand, simply repeat the process on the other side.

The major drawback to the Thai clinch is that you can get into this inside/outside battle, where each person is attempting to gain inside control. To engage in such a battle for long is pointless. For that reason, attempt to establish the inside clinch first and pin it tight. If you have the outside clinch, then attempt to gain the inside clinch quickly, and lock it down tight. If you find yourself in a positional battle, know when it is pointless to continue. Unfortunately, each case will be situation specific, so I cannot tell you when to say when. It takes practice. However, understand that every time the opponent attempts to establish the inside clinch when they have outside, they must remove their grip from you to attempt to reestablish inside. In this moment, you can escape, clamp down hard and start throwing knees, or perform a number of other techniques.

The Push-Off From the Head-Clinch

The push-off is a simple to perform movement that allows you to escape the head-clinch, whether inside or outside. Now, I say simple to perform, because the movement itself is simple. However, it can be hard to perform, if the opponent has a hold of your head in a solid clinch, especially if they are trying to drive your head down. Let me show you the technique.

Figure 111: Again, we start from the head-clinch. It does not matter if you have the inside or outside.

Figure 112: Draw your hand in toward the ribcage of the opponent...

Figure 113: then drive your hand into the ribcage to "push off" the opponent, while at the same time pushing off your front foot. As you push off, you will duck your head under the arms of the opponent.

Figure 114: Use the push off to step out and away from the opponent. Note that you are not pushing the opponent away, but rather using the hands to keep the opponent back while stepping out of the clinch.

Figure 115: Return to stance.

A few quick notes about the Push-off from the Head-clinch. The "push" part is meant to push you away from the opponent and to keep them from moving forward as you duck out and move back. You are not "shoving" them away from you. Think of it as when you do a push up compared to when you shove someone in anger. Additionally, when you step back, you will push off whichever foot is forward. When squared up (both feet even), push off whichever foot is natural to do so.

Other Techniques from the Head-Clinch

You can perform other movements from the head-clinch. "Dragging" your opponent is one technique that I think is underutilized. When the head moves, the body follows. For example, if someone grabs you by the head and forcefully pulls it forward and down, your body will follow behind. With enough force, you can be dragged to the ground in this manner. This is what I am referencing when I speak of dragging the opponent. You may also hear it referred to as "snapping" the opponent down. It is a control technique. There are subtle nuances involved such as wrist angle, forearm position, and other factors best suited for a live training session. However, this is something you can practice on your own.

Strikes from the Body-Clinch

There will be no focus on throwing strikes from the body-clinch, as it is impractical. While one arguably could do this, the angle of the body in accordance with the opponent's body makes strikes awkward, at best. In all reality, you leave yourself open to a number of strikes, when you have the body-clinch, so you do not want to stay in this position for long. Instead, seek to improve position immediately. Since you went for the body-clinch, the assumption is that you want to take it to the ground.

Takedowns from the Body-Clinch

The head-clinch or body-clinch open up the possibility for a takedown. While the body-clinch is the obvious choice, due to the close proximity to the opponent's legs, the head-clinch can lead into a takedown as well. I will focus on the double-leg and single-leg from the body-clinch, as it is ideal for these types of takedowns.

Body-Clinch to Double-Leg

Figure 116: The body-clinch to double-leg takedown is a simple technique to learn, but can be hard to execute against a resistant opponent. You start from the body-clinch. Arguably, you can start from any place with the body-clinch, low, mid, or high, but the best chance of success comes when you are close to the legs. Less distance to travel equals less response time for your opponent.

Figure 117: You start facing your opponent.

Figure 118: You fake a punch to get the opponent to block.

Figure 119: You shoot in and execute the body-clinch.

Figure 120: From the body-clinch, change levels by dropping straight down. You will need to loosen your hands/arms to do this.

Figure 121: From here you execute the double-leg as you normally would, gripping behind the knees, pushing forward into the opponent's hips, and driving them to the ground.

Once on the ground you have effectively completed the body-clinch to double-leg. If you have timed it right and caught the opponent off-guard, you may be able to immediately pass his or her guard and move right into mount or side control. I personally usually aim for side control, because it is easier to pass the one leg, and I like working from side control.

You might question why a person would opt for this as opposed to just going for the double-leg or single-leg. There could be any number of reasons. Perhaps a person does not feel they are quick enough to get the double/single. Perhaps that person fears catching a knee to the face. Regardless of the reason, this technique can be a fine addition to your arsenal.

You can also work in the double-leg from the clinch in other situations. Play with it and see what works.

Body-Clinch to Single-Leg

I may actually prefer the single-leg to the double-leg. There is nothing wrong with the double-leg. but a skilled opponent can grab your neck, if it is to the outside and sometimes even to the inside. Even some of the best wrestlers and takedown artists in MMA fall victim to this. Additionally, with the single-leg, I can turn the corner to drop them on their butt and, since I already have control of a leg with both arms, as the opponent drops, I can step right into side control.

Figure 122: You start facing your opponent.

Figure 123: You fake a punch to get the opponent to block.

Figure 124: You shoot in and execute the body-clinch.

Figure 125: From the body-clinch, change levels by dropping straight down. You will need to loosen your hands/arms to do this.

Figure 126: Instead of grabbing both legs, you grab one. You grab the one leg with both hands/arms and lift it upward. From here, you perform the single-leg as you normally would. You can try to drive forward in order to dump the opponent on their butt. I prefer to turn the

corner and take their supporting leg out from under them. Some people have the ability to bounce very well on one leg when moving laterally. However, most people will fall, if you spin them off their supporting leg. Again, I try to move immediately to side control.

While I am not going to show images for it at this point, a number of moves are possible from side control. From this position, you can mount, sit in scarf, go for a mounted crucifix, and more.

Body-Clinch to Back Control to Takedown

When performing this next move, you will start with the body-clinch on an opponent. You will duck under their arms and rotate to their back. From here, you can drag them to the ground into back control. This move can be ideal, if you fear an opponent catching you in choke during the double-leg or believe that the person has a guard that you do not want to enter.

Figure 127: This technique again starts from the body-clinch.

Figure 128: Stepping first with the foot closet to the direction you wish to step, you move toward the side of your opponent, loosening your grip slightly to facilitate movement, but not releasing altogether. As you move, duck under the arms of the opponent. You continue stepping until you have the opponent's back.

Figure 129: From this position, you essentially begin to sit down. However, you do not sit straight down, but instead sit down at an angle.

Figure 130: As you drive yourself downward, drag your opponent with you, pulling them toward your legs. You do not simply want to

pull them on top of you. As you sit down and pull the opponent into your legs, throw your legs up and wrap them around the opponent. Once you are on the ground, ideally you want to place your legs in a body triangle or simply hook the legs with your feet to hold your opponent in place. You can hook your ankles together, but people generally frown on this, since there is a counter to this leg positioning. However, the counter is rarely used and somewhat weak.

Simple Clinch Combos for MMA

These next combos will not just be combos thrown from the clinch. The **1-2, head-clinch to straight knees to double-leg**, for example, will start from a distance and allow you to establish the clinch, strike from the clinch, and then take the fight to the ground.

1-2, Head-Clinch to Straight Knees to Double-Leg (Not Pictured)

This combos starts from the striking position. Throw the 1-2 (jab-cross) combo, throw the jab again, then fake with a cross, but instead establish the head-clinch (as shown in the clinch section). Throw two knees (this could be one knee off each leg or two knees off one leg), then drop down for the double-leg, press forward to complete the double-leg, and pass into side control. You have now completed the combo and have side control. From here, you can do a variety of moves that we will further go into in Submissions and Striking on the Ground. You can also easily substitute the singe-leg for the double-leg in this combo.

Jab to Body-Clinch to Back Control to Rear-Takedown to Rear Naked Choke (Not Pictured)

You again start from the striking position. You throw the jab to draw your opponent's hands high, then shoot in and establish the body-clinch. Spin to the back and drag the opponent to the ground. You now have the back control from the ground. From here, you can apply the rear-naked-choke. If the opponent is defending well, soften them up with a few punches to the side of the head and face to get them moving, which should create openings to finish the choke.

Other Combos

The preceding combos are just two example of possible combos you can use that incorporate the clinch. Here are some additional combos, sans images.

With the head-clinch established:
Two straight knees to the gut to create space, throw the hook to the body with one hand while maintaining

head control with the other, throw the uppercut to the face, re-clinch and throw two more knees.

Two straight knees to the body, head-drag takedown.

Section Review

Before moving to the strikes or takedowns from the clinch, be sure to have a solid understanding of the clinch. Thoroughly practice establishing and then controlling/keeping both the head-clinch and the body-clinch. Carefully practice the strikes from the clinch once you have done this. Safe practice is key for longevity and practice, practice, practice is what will make you good.

Section 3: Takedowns

This section is going to be a short one. I provided examples of takedowns from the clinch in Section Two, the previous section. Additionally, you will learn how to do the double-leg and single-leg takedowns from the striking position. I will also include defensive maneuvers that you can incorporate into your training to prevent people from taking you down.

Double-Leg Rakedown

The double-leg takedown is a traditional wrestling move that has been adapted to MMA and jiu-jitsu, as well as other arts. The double-leg operates by cutting the person's knees out from under them and applying directional force to make them fall over the cut knees, as you saw in the previous section. Here I will show you how to set up the double-leg from a distance.

Figure 131: Start from the striking stance. Fake a punch and then drop down and shoot forward, aiming to position your shoulder at about hip height of your opponent. You will push off your back foot to move forward initially.

Figure 132: In this image, I have established the position needed to complete the takedown. My hands are behind the knees of my partner, where they will "cut" her balance. My shoulder

is at her hip. When I push forward, this time off my front leg, this will be the contact point for the power.

Figure 133: Having pushed off my front leg, I am now in mid-drive.

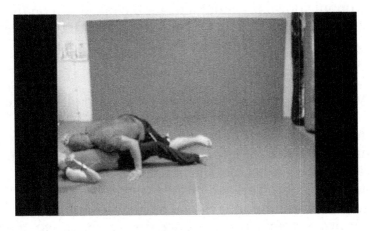

Figure 134: I complete the takedown and land in her guard.

I can stay here and work, but I prefer to pass immediately to side control. To do so, I have my hands on the ground. I push off my hands slightly, while hopping my legs over her leg and jumping into side control. Once I land in side control, I grab her head with my hand/arm closest to her head and grab her leg with my other hand/arm. Other people may place their arms differently, but this is my preference. It keeps the opponent from shrimping away from me, as I have control of the upper and lower body simultaneously, while applying pressure in the middle.

The double-leg takedown varies in its exact dynamic, based on the height of the initiator and the height of the opponent. For example, a shorter person will not need to drop down as far or have as wide a base to compete the takedown on a taller opponent. Conversely, the taller opponent may have trouble dropping down far enough to get the takedown on the shorter opponent. You will have to play with the move to find what is the best depth and base (leg/foot) position for you.

Additionally, passing into side control and placing the hands/arms where I do may work for you, but you may prefer different placement. Play around with it to find what works best for you. One last note is that you can shoot your head to the inside when performing the double-leg. This can protect your neck from a guillotine counter, but can be more awkward to perform for some people. Since there is the threat of the guillotine counter, you want to perform this move as quickly as possible to catch the opponent by surprise.

Single-Leg

The entry to the single can be performed the same as the double-leg. The only difference is that you will shoot for one leg instead of two.

Figure 135: Start from the striking stance...

Figure 136: Throw a punch (again, I am using the jab but another strike could work as well)...

Figure 137: Drop down as you did for the double, shooting forward as you do...

Figure 138: Instead of reaching your hand/arms behind both legs, you will go two on one, reaching for the front leg.

Figure 139: Once you have secured the front leg, you will cradle it with both arms and lift...

Figure 140: Then turn the corner and drop the opponent on their butt. Keep in mind this all should happen very quickly.

Figure 141: You follow the opponent to the ground. I prefer to pass into side control immediately.

With the single-leg, you could just dump the opponent on their butt and not follow them to the ground. This may be ideal if you are in a competition that allows ground stomps or soccer kicks. Additionally, this may be ideal in a street situation where you want to take the opponent down and remove yourself from the scene or have a second opponent to contend with.

Trips, Throws, and Other Takedowns

There are a number of other trips, throws, and similar takedowns that are useful in MMA. Unfortunately, in my humble opinion, there are intricacies to each that will be lost in text, without dedicating a large section to them, which will be beyond the constraints of this manual. However, I want to note that whenever you can get your opponent off-balance and block a foot, you have the potential to take them down. This is something to keep in mind as you clinch up, in the head-clinch or the body-clinch. For example, if you have the head-clinch and pull the person toward you and to the side, you can stick your foot out and trip them. If you have the body-clinch, you can do an inside or outside leg trip. This applies to many different positions, so be on the lookout for opportunities and be inventive.

Takedown Defense

Takedown defense is essential to MMA. There is no way around it. You might be the best striker in the world; but it does not matter, if you are on your back. There are many different defenses to a takedown, but I am just going to go over a few simple ones. Before I do, the most important thing to note in defense, both in general and against takedowns, is movement. Proper movement and evasion tactics can stifle an opponent's attacks. For example, if an opponent shoots forward for a double, you quick step backwards to get out of their range, side step out of range, or quickstep backwards and circle out. If the opponent cannot get a hold on you, he or she cannot take you down. It really is just that simple. Unfortunately, some opponents are just as quick as or quicker than you are, or have impeccable distraction tactics.

Palm-Stop and Forearm-Stop

Figure 142: The palm-stop places your palms on the shoulders of an opponent shooting for a takedown. Start squared up with your training partner.

Figure 143: Your partner then shoots in for a double-leg or a single-leg.

Figure 144: To stop their forward progress, you simple stick your hands out and place them on the shoulders of your opponent. Be sure to have your rear-foot placed solidly back or step back to get a proper base. This gives you a push-off point. If you do not do this, your partner will easily push through you, if they have enough momentum.

Figure 145: From here, you can simply step back, if your opponent has stopped pressing forward.

Figure 146: Alternatively, you can step out and push them to the side.

Figure 147: You can also sink in a choke.

Figure 148: An alternative to the palm stop is the forearm stop. It is the same basic set-up with the exception that you place your forearms on the shoulder of your training partner. You can also do a one-armed stop with the palm or forearm.

The Knee to the Face (Not Pictured)

Another move that I do not use, but that I think it excellent for takedown defense, is the knee to the face/head. When a grappler shoots in for a double-leg and you slam your knee into their face, it has a high probability of knocking them out, hurting them, or at least making them rethink the takedown.

Guillotine Counter (Not Pictured)

Another takedown defense that I absolutely hate, but that is very effective, is the guillotine counter to the double-leg. I do not hate it as a counter; I hate getting caught in it. When I first began grappling, I would always shoot for the double. I had one partner who would always slap this move on me. I cannot count how many times I found myself in the guillotine and had to defend or tap. The worst thing about it is that I outweighed the partner I was working with. Just goes to show you that size and strength are not everything.

Go Heavy

If an opponent does get hold of you with the double-leg or the single-leg, he or she will try to elevate you or take you off-balance to complete the takedown. The most basic defense to this is to go heavy. If the opponent has their hands and body positioned on you for the double-leg, widen your stance, preferably getting one leg back, and weigh down on them. From here, you can do a few things such a push down on their head or grab them around the waist.

Other Takedown Defense

You may notice that I did not include the sprawl. The sprawl is common wrestling defense against takedowns. There is nothing wrong with the sprawl. I do not use this defense. I am not good at it and I am fine with the defense that I have. Just being honest. In addition, I do not mind defending myself off my back. It would not hurt you to learn the sprawl though.

With each of these defenses, except the palm stop, I did not go into a lot of detail. There are certain intricacies of these defenses that I feel make face-to-face learning the best choice for them, or at the very least, a video instruction is better than text.

These defenses as well as other techniques are covered in my other guide **How to Jiu-Jitsu for Beginners**.

Section 4: Grappling

All right, now we get into an area I had to grow to love. Do not get me wrong; I love stand-up striking too. There is something awesome about being punched and punching someone else in the face. I do not always like the getting punched in the face part; but it is definitely an experience.

Grappling is something else. I remember the first time I saw grappling: It bored me. I did not respect the technique on display, but now I do. I look at those same grapplers and anticipate what they are going to do, see how they apply techniques, and sometimes learn something new.

Controlling the Opponent

Control is arguably the single most important aspect of grappling. Now, when I refer to grappling, I mean every aspect of it from the judo to the jiu-jitsu to the wrestling. For me that is grappling. Others may disagree and that is fine. For the sake of this text, think of it in that manner.

Control means what it implies, controlling the situation. This can be grip fighting, positional dominance, maintaining a solid base and other aspects. Any time you are grappling, you should be looking to be in control. Indeed, anytime you are fighting, you should look to be in control. If, when grappling, you are not in control, then the opponent is in control and *they* are leading you where *they* want to go. Now you can use this to your advantage and counter or what not, but really, it is better to take them where *you* want to go.

Teaching control through text is hard, if not impossible. I can offer you techniques; but control is learned through practice. Knowing how to apply pressure to hold an opponent in place, or the best place to set your foot or hand in a position, is a personal thing that can vary, based on size, strength, skill, and other factors. I will not try to teach you in detail how to control, since I am again expecting that you have previous knowledge, but rather give you some pointers that will help you attain, and keep, control.

Wrist Control

Wrist control is important in grappling, but even more important in MMA, since punches are always a threat. It is infinitely more important, if you are on your back.

Figure 149: In this image, I am in my partner's open guard. She does not have wrist control...

Figure 150: So I can posture up...

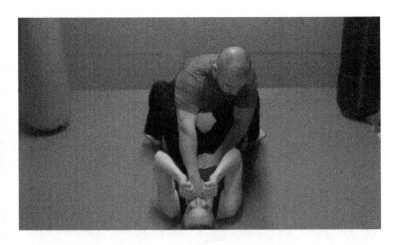

Figure 151: and throw a punch.

Figure 152: Here, instead of lying passively on the ground, to limit punching ability, my partner has taken hold of my arms by the wrists, which can prevent me from throwing a punch. It also sets the stage for her to set up submissions off her back.

Figure 153: Note that there are two different basic ways to have wrist control. The first is one-on-one, as presented in this image, with one hand on each of the opponent's hands.

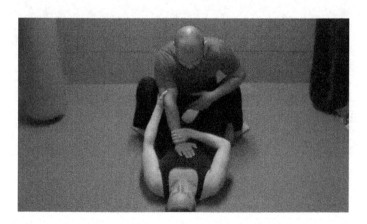

Figure 154: Two-on-one is another option. In this image, you can see that my partner has placed both her hands on one of my arms, although both are not actually on the wrist.

One is instead on the wrist and one on the elbow.

Two-on-one can be ideal, if the opponent is stronger and you cannot go one-on-one. It is also effective, if your opponent is in a more dominant position such as the rear naked. From the rear-naked-choke position, with an opponent on your back, two-on-one controls the choking arm of the attacker. This helps prevent that person from sinking in the choke. Two-on-one can be a problem in some positions. For example, if the attacker is in guard and the defender has a two-on-one defense, the attacker has a hand free to punch. This is clearly not ideal. However, if used to transition to another move such as the arm drag, two-on-one can still be beneficial from such a position. For example, a defender can use the arm-drag to draw the attacker in to obtain head-and-arm control.

Again, I am not going to go into detail on wrist/arm control. That gives you an idea though. If you find yourself in a position close enough for your opponent to punch you, and you are not controlling their arms, they will likely punch you in the face. To avoid that, keep control of their posture and wrists. The head and arm control above is a good example of that; but far from all-inclusive of how to control the posture and arms. For example, in the above images, the techniques were done with an open guard, but the closed guard is best for stopping an opponent from posturing up.

Remember that control is important regardless of position. One person may argue that it is more important from top, while another argues from bottom. Truly, both arguments would be correct, under certain circumstances. For a person who has a strong top game and is in your guard, control becomes more important for that position at that time. If you are in the guard of someone who has a mean submission game off his or her back, control becomes more important in that position at that time. In some cases, a person may be in your guard and have weak passing or poor punching ability from guard, so control becomes less important in this example. However, control is always important to one degree or another. The minute that you stop thinking that it is, is the minute you risk a weaker opponent submitting you or knocking you out.

Head and Arm Control

Let us talk about head control. Remember, wherever the head goes, the body will follow. This is an important concept for both the clinch and grappling. In the following images, all of the techniques come from the closed guard to emphasize the importance of total control. When combined with the closed guard, these head and arm control techniques can completely tie up an opponent. This effectively shuts down their offense, while allowing you to determine your offense.

Figure 155: In this image, my partner has control of my head as opposed to my arms/wrists. Her back, shoulder, and arm muscles are going to be stronger than my neck. This can be a stronger position for her; especially considering controlling my wrists would be difficult due to the strength differences between us. However, from here, I can place my hands on her chest, push off, and use that strength/leverage advantage to break her grip. This will allow me to create space to initiate ground-and-pound.

Figure 156: As an alternative to the above head control, my partner can reach one arm behind my head and then interlace her hand with her other arm. This is an even stronger position and another type of head control. It makes it very difficult for me to get my hands inside to push off and create space.

Figure 157: Finally, we talk about head and arm control. This simply means to control the head and the arm. My partner has one arm

> wrapped around my neck and another around my arm. While she does not have as tight a control on the head, she does lock up the arm and prevent it from attacking. This can be a good position to set up sweeps from.

Okay, so that is a basic overview of head, arm, and wrist control. Again, this is not all inclusive of the aspects of control. There are number of other techniques and intricacies that go into it. Also, remember that the above techniques work best with a closed guard. With open guard, they are not as effective.

Passing the Guard

After some thought, I have decided to omit passing the guard from this manual. The reason for this is guard passing, in my opinion, is highly personal. There are so many different techniques for breaking the closed guard and passing the open guard. Some people, like my partner, prefer to pass on the ground and others, like myself, prefer to pass standing.

From the ground, a person may pass by trying a big step-over. Think Georges St. Pierre. Others prefer to do a technical pass up the middle, pushing down one leg of the opponent, then sliding their leg up, and then repeating on the other side to achieve mount. Think the Gracies, my partner, and so many other people. Still other people prefer to control the legs, push their head to the side of the opponent's legs, and use their bodyweight to push the opponent's legs to the side and pass into side control. This is one of my go-tos for passing on the ground.

These same variances appear in stand-up passing. Marcelo Garcia and Eddie Bravo use a variety of techniques; one of which is to stand in-guard with leg control, push one knee through, and then step over to side control. Others do a big kick back with the leg, and then do the step over. Still others, like myself, get control of the opponent's legs, powerfully throw the legs to the side then explode to pass into side control.

The variety of passing techniques go on. I feel that passing, more than any other set of techniques is personal to the grappler. A strong person may be able to muscle a pass, whereas a weaker person may rely more on technique. Size, strength, and other factors play a role. Since you should already have a jiu-jitsu background, use what you know and look to find other passes that work to your strengths. If you are an explosive person, use passes that best suit this. If you are a strong person, use passes that work best with that. If you are neither, look for technical passes that allow you to exploit weaknesses in the opponent's game and/or make the best use of leverage.

Submissions and Ground-and-Pound

Although the title for this section is grappling, I have included strikes on the ground, or ground-and-pound, as well. Grappling for MMA must take into account the ability to throw strikes. Always remember to be safe, when practicing the following techniques. Even if you and your training partner do not break a bone with a lock, you can cause serious soreness. Strikes on the ground are particularly dangerous, especially when the person striking has top-mount, as the defender cannot evade as he or she would when standing. Safety first.

The Lead In

Figure 158: You start in stance. You throw a punch, or punches, for your set-up then shoot in for a double-leg...

Figure 159: or single-leg.

Figure 160: If you land in your opponent's guard...

Figure 161: Press down on one the opponent's legs while maintaining your base with the other arm...

Figure 162: Draw your leg on the same side to pass the guard on that side...

Figure 163: and base out with your hand...

Figure 164: then pass in the same manner.

Figure 165: You are now in mount and ready to attack from the top.

Figure 166: The first choice here is to punch someone in the face. Posture up and cock your arm back...

Figure 167: and throw the punch. You can continue this way until the person submits or you knock them out. Remember to keep your base strong and if the opponent tries to bridge you off, to base your hands out. To throw a hook from the top, the overall idea is the same.

Elbows From Mount-Top

Figure 168: Elbows can be a little trickier to land. This is due to the rotation of the body that must occur to throw round elbows and the weird angle that 12-6 elbows travel. I prefer round elbows and those are what we will review. You can start from tight to your opponent in mount.

Figure 169: From here, you cock the arm back by slightly rotating your body and arm away from the opponent...

Figure 170: then reverse the rotation to slam the elbow into the opponents face. This can start and execute in a variety of ways. Play around and find the best way for you to hold top position and throw elbow from the mount.

Use extreme caution when practicing ground-and-pound with a real person. If you have a focus mitt, Thai pad, or even a suitcase pad that you can use as a target, use it. Have the partner on the ground hold it in the target position. If you do opt to perform these techniques without a pad of some sort, use gloves for punches and elbow pads for elbows. Additionally, you should stop short from actually making contact with the opponent. The gloves or elbow pads are just in case you fail to stop short.

Americana from Mount

The Americana, or key-lock, is a staple in jiu-jitsu submissions. It involves rotation of the shoulder. While you are punching or elbowing your opponent in the face, they may extend their hands out to stop you. It is at this time that the opportunity to perform the Americana is present.

Figure 171: In this image, my partner is throwing punches.

Figure 172: To defend against these punches, I extend my hands.

Figure 173: At this point, she reaches across with her opposite arm to attack the arm on which she wants to perform the Americana.

Figure 174: She forces the arm down to ground and allows her elbow to land near the side of my head...

Figure 175: before snaking her other arm underneath and grabbing her own wrist.

Figure 176: She then pulls the arm down in a sweeping motion, while rotating upwards at the elbow to facilitate the cranking of the submission. This is a shoulder lock, but puts pressure on the opponent's elbow as well.

Mounted Crucifix to Punches and Elbows

Figure 177: Again, we are going to start standing, in order to show you how to get to this position.

Figure 178: Fake the punch...

Figure 179: then shoot in for a double-leg...

Figure 180: or single-leg.

Figure 181: Complete the takedown and pass into side control. From this angle, you can see that my partner's leg is next to my arm.

Figure 182: She steps her leg over my arm trapping it. If need be, she can use her arm on the same side to push my arm down to trap it between the leg. It will depend on how your

opponent places his or her arm. You now have the Mounted Crucifix position.

Figure 183: While continuing to stay heavy, she draws her arm back, looking to land her elbow to my face.

Figure 184: She then drives the elbow into my face. This can also be done with a punch. The exact angle and path traveled by the elbow or

punch will vary, based on exact body position and length of limbs.

Other Submissions from Side-Control and Top-Mount

Other submissions I suggest, from side-control and top-mount, include the Forearm Choke from Mount and the Americana from Side Control. You essentially perform the Americana from Side-control in the same manner as the Americana from Mount. You perform the Forearm Choke from Mount simply by jamming your forearm into the opponent's throat, to restrict blood flow or to apply pressure to the trachea. For that reason, I did not illustrate it, because it really is that simple in my opinion. As always, practice safely. Additionally, you can perform an Americana or Straight Arm-lock from the Mounted Crucifix. This is just a sampling of possible moves. Refer back to your jiu-jitsu training or reference secondary sources for further instruction, including but not limited to my other guide **How to Jiu-Jitsu for Beginners**.

The next area to be covered is attacking from the guard. Being able to defend and attack from your back is an essential aspect of surviving a fight that goes to the ground. Most times, when a fight ends up on the ground, the attacker ends up mounting the defender or ends up in the guard of the defender. A strong guard can neutralize punches and submissions from the attacker, while setting up attacks for the defender.

Arm Bar from Guard

Figure 185: In this image I have a high guard and my hands positioned over my partner's wrists as she holds me down.

Figure 186: In one swift motion, I isolate one arm, push her head to the side and rotate my hips.

Figure 187: I bring my legs together. I kept this loose in this image to prevent too much pressure on my partner's arm.

Figure 188: I extend, pushing my hips upward to hyperextend the arm. For practice purposes, I kept my legs loose, otherwise my knees would be in tighter and I would extend more.

Figure 189: As you extend, the opponent may fall. He or she will fall toward open space where the arm is trapped.

Figure 190: Go with the opponent as he or she falls. This may even drag you into an upright position as noted here. Keep control of the arm and leg position.

Figure 191: Fall back, extending the arm and pushing the hips skyward to complete the arm bar. Notice that I do not really extend here, in order to save my partner some pain.

Triangle choke from guard

Figure 192: I start with my partner in guard.

Figure 193: I isolate an arm.

Figure 194: In one swift motion, I push the isolated arm back and draw my leg up. Some people step on the hip, first, to create space and gain position. I generally do not.

Figure 195: I bring my other leg up quickly, in order to lock my partner up.

Figure 196: In another swift motion, I isolate her other arm and push my hips skyward, which elevates her, and begin to drag her arm across my waist.

Figure 197: I slide the arm across my waist.

Figure 198: I reach up and grab my foot to close the triangle. Some people do not need to do this. I do.

Figure 199: I pull the ankle down behind my knee. Notice I continue controlling her arm.

Figure 200: I can now apply pressure to the head and complete the choke.

Kimura from Guard

Figure 201: I start in closed guard.

Figure 202: In one swift motion, I isolate one of my partner's arms, open my guard, and begin to sit up toward the isolated arm.

Figure 203: With my opposite hand, I reach behind her arm and grab my own wrist.

Figure 204: I then fall back, twisting my body toward the side where I am attacking. Notice that my legs stay tight on her back and her leg on the opposite side.

Figure 205: I begin to crank the arm up the back. For safety reasons, I crank minimally during this practice session.

The three proceeding moves are very effective techniques off the back. Even if you do not get the submission, an attacker will be wary. Furthermore, these techniques can set up the opportunity for an escape, sweep, or another submission. With an opponent attacking in your guard, sometimes the best defense is a good offense. Do not lose sight of control though. Control and these techniques go hand in hand.

Grappling Combos

Combos in grappling are very different from what you use in stand-up. Generally, you may refer to it, or hear it referred to, as chaining techniques together. The exact meaning can change from one person or school to the next. For me, I refer to the grappling combo as a failed submission attempt that leads into another one seamlessly. For example, if you attempt the triangle and you cannot get it, then you can rotate your hips and attempt the arm bar. If the opponent blocks the arm bar, you can roll into an omoplata (Shoulder lock). If the opponent defends the omoplata, you can often roll right back into the triangle or arm bar, dependent on how the person defends.

Conversely, you can "combo" submission attempts into sweeps or other techniques. For example, if you try the hip-bump sweep from guard and it fails, you can attack with the Kimura. If the Kimura fails, you can scoot out and attack the neck with a guillotine. You may even be able to scoot out from a failed Kimura from guard to a get-up. It really depends on each situation and how the other person responds. Teaching these combos is intricate and beyond the scope of this particular text. However, the purpose of me sharing this is to let you know that combos for grappling are present and applicable to MMA or street fighting. In the best interest of being a complete martial artist, fighter, or person who can defend themselves on the street, you should understand how ground techniques chain together.

The End

The preceding has been an introduction to MMA. I cannot stress enough that you should use this material in conjunction with previous experience in jiu-jitsu and kickboxing. The learning materials, here, rely on your prior understanding of certain techniques, and omits certain techniques that previous basic training in jiu-jitsu and kickboxing will teach.

The lack of prior knowledge in these arts will leave you with holes in your game from the start. For example, I omitted common blocking and evasion movements, as this will be the first thing you learn in any good boxing or kickboxing setting.

Even with the prior knowledge in these areas, there will still be more for you to learn. Where your white belt to blue belt jiu-jitsu course teaches you basic jiu-jitsu, and the beginner kickboxing course teaches you the basics of stand-up striking, this teaches you the basics of how to incorporate those techniques for MMA.

There is always more to learn; but you are on a solid path, if you have all of these lessons behind you. It can take many years to become proficient in any one martial art, let alone the combination of arts found in MMA. Do not rush the process. Take the time and learn the techniques correctly. Be patient with yourself, your partners, and the process as a whole.

Remember that safe training is smart training. Practice techniques in good form to avoid muscle pulls, awkward impacts with heavy bags or other items, and remember that your training partner is just that, your partner. They are not the enemy. You are not training with them to go all out and hurt them. When practicing these techniques early on, you should use the least effective pressure necessary. As time goes on, pressure can increase, but should never exceed 75% in training. Save the 100% power for the ring or the street. Conversely, when caught in a submission, tap early to prevent injury. Being a tough person, in training, is not the best way to keep training. Keeping you and your partner safe will keep you both training longer.

Just the Beginning

As an introduction to MMA, there are certain things missing from this book. Notable omissions include sweeps and defense for grappling. However, as I mentioned multiple times, this book comes as a complement to previous experience. If you lack experience in sweeps and defense for grappling, find a class, video examples, or at least a text. Drill these techniques until they are second nature. Do not worry about fancy moves, but instead stick to the basics early on. The basics are effective and easier for a beginner to learn.

Footwork for striking is another omission. Again, reference the notes on previous experience. If you have poor footwork, find a class or least watch some videos. While it is possible to learn footwork from a text, and I have a text out that includes footwork; it is best learned via an actual moving demonstration. Footwork is the key to managing distance, evading strikes, executing strikes, defending takedowns, initiating takedowns, and overall success in virtually every aspect of MMA or martial arts.

Finally, intermediate to advanced striking, clinch work, and grappling instruction manuals should follow up this text and your previous training outside of this text. I have other manuals out, but they just cover the basics, as I look to educate the beginner. Obviously, a reputable gym can provide intermediate to advanced classes. However, that is not for everyone. If classes do not work for you, there are other options. I am a personal trainer and clearly, I can train you on some of the material, if you are within my range. However, for learning in the digital world and the written world, there are solid options. Cung-le has an in-depth text on San Shou, a martial arts which covers various aspects of MMA. Rener and Ryron Gracie offer some of the Gracie jiu-jitsu coursework online via the virtual Gracie Academy. Duke Roufus and Scott Sullivan offer some excellent kickboxing techniques via in-home and online video programming. There are numerous others as well. Your local Barnes and Noble probably carries a number of the texts, including the text from Cung-le.

There is no replacement for a live course with a competent instructor. However, this does not work for everyone, but you should still seek the advice of someone reputable. Even if you simply join an online program such as Jean Jacques Machado Online Training, MG in Action (Marcelo Garcia), or Tae Kwon Woo (Master Woo), you can interact with trainers and other people in the same place as you. Feedback is essential to the learning process. Find people who can give you feedback that helps you grow. Remember that you must be receptive to this feedback. Clearly, you should not listen to uneducated or undereducated people who try to critique you; but you should listen to people with skill levels greater than yours, in areas you are trying to learn. This does not mean you should never question what they say. Indeed, ask plenty of questions. However, if you just choose to question needlessly as a form of argument or refusal of their advice, then you are doing yourself a disservice. You will not always hear positive things and you will not always like what you hear. Take the good with the bad, in order to grow. I have worked with USAPL Powerlifters, jiu-jitsu black belts, taekwondo black belts, and other skilled people. I still learn today and sometimes hear things I do not like. It is all part of the process.

Moving forward, I wish you the best possible success. Be proud yet humble in all the things that you do and remember to pay it forward.

Recommended Resources

- HowExpert.com – Quick 'How To' Guides on All Topics from A to Z by Everyday Experts.
- HowExpert.com/free – Free HowExpert Email Newsletter.
- HowExpert.com/books – HowExpert Books
- HowExpert.com/courses – HowExpert Courses
- HowExpert.com/clothing – HowExpert Clothing
- HowExpert.com/membership – HowExpert Membership Site
- HowExpert.com/affiliates – HowExpert Affiliate Program
- HowExpert.com/writers – Write About Your #1 Passion/Knowledge/Expertise & Become a HowExpert Author.
- HowExpert.com/resources – Additional HowExpert Recommended Resources
- YouTube.com/HowExpert – Subscribe to HowExpert YouTube.
- Instagram.com/HowExpert – Follow HowExpert on Instagram.
- Facebook.com/HowExpert – Follow HowExpert on Facebook.

Made in the USA
Middletown, DE
23 August 2020